Time Calluses

Lee Poechmann

Acknowledgment

Throughout the years, I have received valuable encouragement and criticism that furthered my writing. In addition to my teachers and professors, who made me write (or read) when I would rather draw, in particular, I want to thank Carolyn Mayer, Debra Nardi, Gaye Shipman, Robert Eckley, and Bob McDonald for shaping me in my youth.

I am grateful to the Horsemen---Cabell Vest, Justin Green, Chip Edwards---for their source of adventures, brotherhood, perspective and letters; to Jamie Small for bobcats, sparkles and sharing; Heather Brown Holleman for your positivity and God-centered life; Marianne Desmarais for coalescing art and architecture into a poetic worldview; Al Ip for twenty-five years' of probing conversations on culture and zeitgeist; Michelle Kindy for listening patiently without judgment to my obsessions; and the Catholic Writers' Guild - St. Johns Chapter for consistent, faithful support.

I thank my parents, Jim and Harriet Poechmann, for a strong family unit built on openness and love, and my brother, Barry, who only becomes more important in my life with each passing year. I love you.

Contents

Sunday, August 3

Foreward

In July 2014, my job was not going well. Still adjusting to life after divorce, I felt socially isolated, spiritually unbalanced. Free weekends were rare, as a parent, and I was cash strapped.

To kick the funk, I designed an especially eventful summer weekend with friends and adventures. I was looking forward to it for weeks.

Upon its approach, on Thursday afternoon, my weekend fell apart: everyone and everything I had planned for Friday, Saturday, and Sunday canceled on me.

The previous day, I received an invitation to my friend's art show opening in New Orleans, and for a scant ten seconds, considered the ludicrous excursion: an eight-hour drive to New Orleans for the exhibit gala, knowing I may not even get five minutes with my friend, who I had not seen in fourteen years.

At 5pm Friday, I left work and hit the road heading west. This is my catalog.

Friday, August 1

Thank You

Thank you, friends
For saying no
Sending me out
The forcing of my hand
Generous gerunds
Away from comfort
Where no means yes.

I-10 West Approaching Live Oak

It sneaks up, mile by mile
Pace carefully calibrated
Slow, growing
Furious when required, then measured
Stalking
Painfully loving and obsessive
The only
Way. Will it take by day or by night?

In the Zone

Feel it coming
Triggered back then
Decisions to make and never look back
Dissipate like static discharge
Next trumps last
Agitate to frenzy
Then surrender to
Strange genetics.

Get lost
Uncomfortable
Find limits.

Swell with this sheer wave
A ride to long for
A convergence
Creative orgasm
Time and desire vanish
Absolute concentration
Delivers essence by depth
Not knowing how to get there
Not knowing how to stay
Conjure again
Because there is no formula
It can't be purchased
So drop everything
And revel now.

Wanderlust

Long ago I gave in
Decided when I saw her
        So silly
Then I knew her.
She was the Hanging Gardens of my Mind.

I admit I
Created
And felt and projected
And swam blind her mapless caverns
        Lost.

I nourish and foment this aching, unrequited anguish
        I want to know
To ramble new terrain
To fly frozen in her chilly volume
To understand
        Me.

Prepare to Turn Your Watch Back

Unwound
Free
To pic deep into
Nostalgia
Heart-first
And mine the truth
As it was then
And now
After pressure and time
What it has become.

In Short Supply

A fraud in the creative closet
And this is my jailbreak
From impotence.
I waste away
Trying to be responsible
While my soul suffers.
Can I live my life with courage?
Can I give myself that gift?

I belong among fertile fields of
Moving bodies, not a corporate.
God has given me a gift to share.
Yet I am stuck in a sick numbers game
Tax code tar pit.

I am not an employee after all
But a free agent
Who has no agency over his freedom
Journeyman wanderer artist
And if not, I am a fake
Stealing.

How much did she pay you
To build her dream
At the expense of yours?

Guidance Counselor

I come to escape
To study, find answers.
My pilgrimage: I need
Alone, all day long
Overdue.

Can't Hang

My retreat
A polite middle finger
To certain people I know
Who talk big and fall flat
All hat no cattle.
I will out-everything you.

The Road

Unpacking reconciliation
Resolutions
Meditations that can't be accomplished
On my knees
It will design my ascension
Holy highway.
Here is my confessional.

Force Rank

Sometimes
I wonder if it's
Best to be a virgin
Or veteran
First second or
Last?

A Different Way to Heal

I hurt to mend
Trade several single slices
Trolling bumps along bottom
Shallow and uneven, forgettable
For one deep gash
Damaging and glorious
One beautiful scar
Through tender flesh
A brand with a story.
I hurt to mend.

Leo Begat Taurus

I am here to make good
Make up make out
Intellectually
The way we flirted then
Right brained
Fourteen years ago.

I was straitjacketed
By idealism
And you weren't perfect
So I made a mistake
Failed
The cursed of my life.

This is for foreign films
Welding lessons
Michigan autumn
Nina Simone
Hot dogs and tennis
Couches cum car crash...

> Quaking in the median
> Saturday speeding by sponging sobs
> Of totaled now what embracing and
> Wrestling with that always awkward
> Is there something more here than
> Friend consoling friend mixed with
> We are in big trouble police impending
> Punishment and disappointment
> Which is always way worse but there are
> No parents to let down no one to
> Answer these questions quash prickly
> Emotions so neatly so we say nothing

...For the show I said no
The move I never made.
For courage this time
Finally
To watch you live your dream with him.
I think I could have been happy.

Someday Soon

I watch teen girls with their dads
Just their dads, and
I don't know.
Do I want my daughter to be hot
Tan fit pretty curvy
At fourteen
Someone else's dream?
Confident yes and whip-smart too
but grounded, modest. Maybe
I want her to collect all I wasn't
The traits admired and catalogued
Secretly, from the back of the class
Observing
Thinking I could study my way
To safety

Meanderings

Time is elastic
Chasing my moth, changing tense
To future perfect.

Fortune Cookie

If you are
Authentic, you
Possess
Inherent beauty.

I-10 West outside Tallahassee, 7:30pm

Obsession
The healthy splinter
Festers
To focus life be creative.
Paul knew the thorn
Obsession develops the plot.

Laid bare obsession gives great the most
To care about one thing more than anyone else
To see through laser eyes
Our protagonist who can't avoid the exhaustive effort
To know all
Savant-like
Inhabit the subject
Climb inside
And show from a place we can never stand.

Live a thesis you never tire of
Prove your pearl
Diver immersed
A conspiracy of desire a masterwork
Fiction infatuation
Twist the doorknob and be mine.

Through uber you live.
And after all this
What do you do
Go
Put to work?

Death is in Season

Death is in season now
Collected in bunches
Heaping grief upon grief in our basket.
Children spouses
Pantry mouses
Wherefore cries the brood.
Death is yes
But that's not too vex
Abrupt. Absolute.
Death is fear no let
At sunrise our father
What do we do with the body
At sunset? Unknown
Can be a temporary moment
Surmounted
And yet
Forever is only forever.

I-10 West, Nighttime

Zoning I don't see
People or cars. I don't hear
Sounds. No one can touch me
Can't hit me with anger.
The road is my sanctuary, a
Bubble and shield
Devoid of all superfluous.
Me a car and my thoughts.
I drive my thoughts
My thoughts the car
And the car drives me.

Roadside Inn Room 200, Marianna

Posh hotels are nice
Appropriate for business
Immaculate comfortable unwanting.

When the work is done
Pound pavement
Trade perfection
And shimmering sapphire pool for

A murky tin pit
To cleanse weary paraffin souls
And frighten the frass
Honest gaudy and stained inventory
Laminated for quick wipe down
Where guests carpet furniture
Matted oily and mismatched
Respectively
An untouchable appliance
Snickers over skin

Fit
Where headlights trace three pocked walls
War atrocities
Babies wail dogs bay
A frigid queen slabbed stiff
With hospital corners, handicraft
Jarring aberration

Where a scowling condenser
Is moist music
To play poker with bedbugs
Raskolnikov would
Recalibrate to reality
Tenderly
Ice, life out of order.

Saturday, August 2

The Cold Side of the Pillow

After creative contortions and
Barrel rolls to find fatigue
I give up and defeated
In these early dark hours
And write.

I swap fetal for adult
Serotonin for cortisol
Scarlet sclera
Sprinting heart
Teeth grinding
In conscientious objection.

Why not go on
Tilt with antagonizing zeal---
Fuck polite---
And say how it is
More importantly
How it will be?
Dictate life
My Way finally.

Everything worthy should be
All fetid and complete
Psychosis
Why not win the companion story
Consolation prize
And game too a good night's sleep?

Touchstone

This trip an itch
Long time a'comin'
Professional course correction.

Live your life by momentum
Days clocks math and route
By God. History has no place here.

I-10 West toward Crestview

Follow a line
White and broken
Paired with another
Yellow and constant.
They are dissimilar but mated
Independently whole but
Complementary.
They work in tandem.

They teach guard and guide
Freight and folly
Folly and freight
Through verdancy
Consolation and desolation
Planar and spatial
Specifically high and generically low.

We have but a few miles
To learn the laws before the lines
Blur and fade
Before the exits
Decisions
All alone are ours.

Modern Hero

Odysseus the beggar
Not me
Is unemployed cash and carry
Cheap driven childless
And without a past.
Nobody's man.
The clothes
Though mere threads
Own this day only
Feed the immediate need
Animalistic ascetic
Apostolic and beat
Soul and God
Essence in the everyday.
Scratch run wonder
Crawl cry hurt claw
To escape
To find anything to escape.

Escambia Bay, Early Morning

Sun hard sweating
Sends fog fleeing
Lifts the satin off
Beach sand and
A summer Saturday begins.

Where I Stand

Me now
Corporate and creative
In conflict.

If I Really Listen...

...God speaks
When my daughter
Derives a truth beyond her years
A surprising non-sequitur
Both tenet later and reality now

Unspoken by me
But modeled and perhaps framed by
Accident
By me.
And I choke.

The miracle craft
Beauty of a brain soul shaping
Knowing I am doing
The best I know how
And even I will be okay.

Own It

I will not deflect and bury blame.
I will not act like it never happened.
I bend to no one but God.

I will embrace and dissect and
Probe and exhibit
This misadventure.

Then I will watch it
Fade and sink
To the bottom

Like a waterlogged leaf
In a ruddy lake.
Amen.

Water Weight

We set off on
This long ocean swim
Only allowed a brief spell to
Tread water and catch our breath with
No land in sight.

So many drown
Disoriented in the dark
Swimming deeper to depth
Unable to churn arms and legs
In routine
Because the water is ice and
What we really need is not rescue
Nor partner direction
But sabbath, buoy.

Mantra

A simple edict:
Live and let die---what it takes
To last a lifetime.

Team Building

You must earn unlimited devotion
Elephant faithful
Ex ex ex ex
Extend and then collapse.
Too many times.
Sh sh sh sh
Shame on me.
Prove to me you belong.
Reciprocate
Your interest care
With with with with
Love or thought or prayer or hello
Or be gone.

Muscle Memory

This excursion most resembles my
College road trips, days on the road
When destination trumped the task at hand
Anything academic.

Old friendships hostage to entropy
Can thaw now every day possible
Anew from God to stand on its own
A microcosm of life.

The passenger promoted to driver, exercises
Feelings atrophied by years
Caked with neglect, muscled with fear
But cowardly no more.

Escatawpa Bayou, Late Morning

Mother tongue of love pray
Don't give me away.
Tease tickle
And when you get a giggle
Smile like she does
And extend your hand
Like she does
For a truce a touch
And maybe a kiss
Like she may
Someday.

Upon Entering the Parish

Where is my rich family lore
Complicated and human
Of love---God self other---
The stories people pay dearly to read
Pray fearly to leave?
They are rare coins
Sticky mothy vernacular and verbal
Passed down fabled and don't fit
So neatly into an album frame
Or banker's box.
I want a life's worth of those.

Days Inn Room 202, Metairie

Tonight will defy expectation
Fashion and art history
Skin and smiles and mystery
Possibility
Will collide
Without my control
For this night is not mine
This night
Was manifest
Long ago. I go
To swallow
So I may reconcile guilt
Love
And things much more still life
Than that.

I will arrive to excise the bad
Rewrite with good
Mourn
To see an alternate future
One I could have lived
If I had no blind curves or dead ends
No poetic ghosts to chase
Alas.

Homage to Shel Silverstein

It knew something once
But it wasn't good
So it tried to forget it.
But it hurt
Not because it knew something
But because of everything it didn't yet know
And because knowing that one thing
Meant it couldn't know everything else.
And the one thing it knew
Wasn't even true
So
Maybe it never really knew anything at all.

Life as I See It

Every day is a struggle

To be Holy Getting nearer to God

Is a fight against most everything.

Holiness is a peaceful

Awe-inspiring accomplishment

A cloud view

from a mountain top.

One fights with prayer

Work

Puritanical at times---

And the Way

is never so clear.

Love is hard

Being open to God

is harder.

Cold for Your Soul

Fanning like a tourist
Locals learn to swelter
Steam smolder
Inside
To outgrace their sweat.
Cool is a state of mind.

White Linen Night

On this eve Saturday
White linen language
Is the spoken reason
To rendezvous in the dusk.
Second line elegance
Given shape and color
Clean comfort classy
Southern ladies and gentlemen coast
Past pealing bell towers
Past mellifluous music
Draped in the ripe cotton air.
On Julia a spiritual glow
Angelic and alight
A counterpoint and foil
To the notorious inferno
Yon Bourbon.

City Proper and the French Quarter

She offered an intimate peek,
Centipeding alleys and gardens
Mysterious, demure tattoos
Antiquities, Cartesian scripts
Art and well-detailed were her clothes.

Her overt style celebrated with every move
Under planter boxes, as we paraded
Dodging filigree, tempting with jazz, seducing with voodoo
Dressed rough and ready in her madras of brick
Tile wood iron stone and stucco.

As we progressed, dancing
Around the levees, a glance at a time
Old in a new way, into the steamy maze…

No disguise was unknown.
Everyone fits her profile, mired in excess
Still a voyeur's subject was I, all night…

I was torn tropical
Soaking in her bayou, overcome. She
Washed over me, spilling through my pores
Percolating wildly
Too much to absorb, she came
From the inside, from all directions.

Gas lamps wiggled, entrancing
Hindering my retreat from standing gutters---
Sweat, spit, seed, spew---too human
Nothing a deluge could not rain away.
I sought a nook of escape, prayed for her
Then climbed the walls.

Ogden Museum, Fifth Floor, 7:30pm

In the gallery
Sepia hair gesso skin
Scanning blending
And failing. Tailspin
Alone in the crowd like me.

Art as a backdrop to her
Aura
Afraid to smile afraid
To flirt no eyes
And I had an alibi.

I was looking for courage.
She was looking for me
Was she
And again
I never found we.

Sunday, August 3

Missing Person

To know a person's routine
Days of the same
An amore you adore
From afar or just a pleasant smile
Amidst the oarwork of your day
Where she could be should be
You can be
Disappointed
When you count on it that one day
When you need it
And she is missing.

Then maybe searching
Or forgetting
Going about your business
With no expectation you see her
And it amazes.
Of all the places
Observed in the most democratic way

Parked on a street, which could be any street
In a large city, which could be any city
Running an errand, which could be any errand
At this time, which could be any time

Of all the places in the world two people
Can share the same square yard of Earth
Paces unplanned
And it's a little gift
A serendipity thank you
God at my service again
And a good day becomes great.

Lee Poechmann

For M.D.

I should not
But I do
Live through
Not
The rich or famous or handsome or lucky
But through courage
Those who have more than me
Willing to unbalance
Get uncomfortable and wobble---
Who took a risk and succeeded
Who have done what I have
Not not yet yet someday.

Sunday Sunrise

She will gaze out over the Mississippi
To Algiers' toothy
I-told-you-so grin
Trying to absorb last night's revelry

Enabling countless walks of
Shame
Hung over
Then submit to a douche.

Seagull
Barge
Street car
Chime.

A photographer scurries along brick
Like a wharf rat
Attempting to capture naked honesty
Before she awakes.

Tale of Two Cities

Sly courtyard secrets
Behind the scenes New Orleans
Not tourist fodder.

Home Soon

Wake scales piles claps stone
Bank---Gulf memories resist
Time to go, August.

French Quarter Cleanup

Motorized vacuum mobiles
Street sweeper machines
Brooms mops
Hoses power washers
Trash bags cans dumpsters garbage trucks
Mechanical pickers---
All in steep service
This day of rest
Overlooking polished
Eschewing antiseptic
To find something less than disgust.

St. Louis Cathedral, 9am

Outsiders hear this institution
Stale and rigid, traditional
Old ways un-hip
Behind the times---even haughty.
They think they know the Catholic Church.

But do they know
Soup kitchens, homeless shelters
Sanctuaries, immigrant assistance
Orphanages, marriage preparation
Halfway homes, counseling
Cemeteries, military chaplains?

Do they know the
Primary and secondary schools
Universities and research
Tuition scholarships
Healthcare
Support groups
And social ministries
Foundations and charities
Adoption agencies and human rights lobby
Donations, volunteers, utility amnesty---
Much of it free
No questions asked?

This Church is open and welcome to all
The safety net of society
All in service of the immediate and dire
And yet building for the future.

Do they feel God at work in their lives?
Or are they too busy building a case
To criticize...method?

If you have ever needed
Been broken by life, lost
You have known what it's like
To be catholic
Universal.

Dixie Bolero (Redux)

A time to escape
Look for native sway
Partner elegant and refined
Floating amongst stone
Efflorescent in the light
Answers to questions yet unposed
A pilgrimage to find a parasol

> I needed to prowl
> Wander in a mad fit
> With a guide neurotic and teetering
> Afield sweat riveted on her brow
> Tittering to search in séance
> Ten times for the same thing
> And never find it

A debutante newly uncloistered
In the delta daybreak she
Was a stately magnolia
Lording over her garden
Well-detailed spilling white linen
Centipeding allées and grid shifts

> Stain of the south on her roux
> Garter bridges béton brut
> Rolling cameo of creamy café
> To skinny-dip in a half moon
> Her coquettish style celebrating every move
> Under planter boxes we paraded

Mysterious demure room to room
I dove through jalousie anonymous to see
Antiquities Cartesian scripts
As we progressed coasting
Around the levees a glance at a time

Dodging filigree tight with jazz tempting voodoo
Plowing a rough and ready madras of materiality
Clay and ceramic ferrous and stucco
Wood no disguise unknown
Her profile a fit to each mired in excess

She offered an intimate peek
Past pealing bell towers
Old in a new way into the steamy maze
I was torn tropical

A reason to multiply in the dusk
Robust fleshy shelter of sin
Still a voyeur's subject was I all night
Gas lamps wiggled entrancing

Soaking in her bayou overcome. She
Washed over me spilling through my pores
Percolating wildly

Hindering my retreat from her inferno
Sweat spit seed standing in gutters too human
Nothing a deluge couldn't rain away

Too much to absorb she came
From the inside

I sought a nook of escape
Prayed for her

From all directions.

Then climbed the walls.

I-10 East Toward Bonifay, 4:15pm

Pace posse peloton
    Alternating wind breaking
        Overtaking
Like a swarm of yellow jackets
    Lions of the Serengeti
        Devouring terrain and wildebeest

Neutral the camouflage
    Of modernity exposed
        Vistas on a Mobius strip
A video game of sorts
    No rabbits no radar
        We move as conditions allow.

Despite traps and pranks
    The pack has rules
        Communal mores and unspoken respect
Even at high speed---
    Anything to stave boredom
        And regret

From the 300-mile gauntlet
    We ride fast and tap history
        Lawrence's Bedouin
On dromedaries to Damascus
    Fighting heat's snaky dance
        Running to drink our mirage.

Lee Poechmann was born and raised in Williamsport, Pennsylvania, has lived in six states, and visited thirty-four others. He began writing poetry as a travel log on his trips around Europe while studying in Finland, and continues to be inspired by travel and exploration. As an architect, Lee is drawn to classical beauty, and both natural and man-made wreckage---worn, authentic, unglamorous---and is interested in how our built and social environments collide. When in the city, he enjoys finding neighborhoods and good food on foot; when in the country, he seeks out hikes and routes less travelled---and prefers a road trip to flight, train, or boat to get there. *Time Calluses* is Lee's first book.